FOUR FOR FOUR

FOUR FOR FOUR

WK LAWRENCE

BROKEN TRIBE PRESS

Four for Four
Copyright © 2024 William K. Lawrence
First Edition

Paperback ISBN: 9781965412480

Library of Congress Control Number: 2024925342

Gratitude to the following journals for publishing early versions of these poems: *Berkley Poetry Review, Eno, Paragon Journal, Pen Himalaya, Rue Scribe, Straight Forward, Stoneboat Review, Underwood Press*, and *Vending Machine Press*.

Published by Broken Tribe Press
Lawrence Landing Company
Raleigh, North Carolina 27609
USA, North America

Broken Tribe Press is a proud member of:

Independent Book Publishers Association
    and
Community of Literary Magazines and Presses

www.brokentribepress.com

BROKEN TRIBE PRESS

CONTENTS

Passage

You are probably crying on a pillow
staring at the gray walls up and down
until you've counted every nail hole
like a painter waiting with spackle in hand.
It's a place where we all fall into:
the nights are dark and starless,
they wipe the slate clean,
though you may be bent in dream
with the pillow clutched in your hands
squeezed into shapes, perpendicular slants
that close you in safe.
Those sheets hover over your legs
almost held there for a second
by a slight breeze
that reminds you of home.

Leaving Home

Tar under the wheels
Blurring past yellow lines
Crossing bridges
Back onto the main land
As tall shadows of steel loom behind
And the trees sprout up
Replacing the shadows
Ancient bedrock exposed
Up and down the landscape
A warm up in elevation for later
But soon it's all flat again
Corn husks blowing by our faces
Swirling sky turns gray
And we can almost see a little boy
With a feather in his ear
Sitting upon a hill with a bison by his side.
After a while these wheels turn into hooves
And the tar turns to dirt
Only the growing elevation pulls us back
To a world behind a windshield
Sweating, straining, burning more fuel
Snow begins to pelt the glass
And it looks like we're flying through space
Stars rushing by as we come off that mountain
Tall shadows of majestic snow-capped peaks
Loom in the rear-view mirror,
We travel parallel to a gorge
In and out of a valley
To the ocean and we won't stop.

The Plumber

If I could go back and do it all over again.
I'd be a plumber instead of a poet.
I'd be a plumber instead of a professor too.

The plumber doesn't have a glamourous title
but the necessity of their job demands respect
and good money too!

Plumbers have an enormous waitlist
of anxious clients
praying for their arrival,
dependent on the work they do,
relieved and joyful when they leave.

We need the plumber when the pipes freeze or clog,
when a leak springs from the wall,
when the sink or shower ceases.
We need the plumber
with an urgency to cleanse, cook, and drink.

> Imagine the value of such an occupation...
> To really be needed and wanted.

Like a plumber, I place a solution down the pipe,
let it absorb and eat away at the clog,
but as a poet and professor,
I can't force it with a tool.

When it works and I've washed away the clog,
it's always without seeing the fruits of my labor.
I want to see the clog liberated.

I want to see the excrement drain.
I want to see the water flow for once.

I envy the plumber
because they get to see the results
and they get paid more to walk away
knowing they've seen the progress.

As a poet and professor,
I feel like I can't really clear the pipes,
or get the water flowing
or install the necessary fixtures in the home.
Not in a single day.
I can't save the day.

The Ukrainian Baker

The baker is a small man
Without much hair
Without much muscle
But he has heart and skill
And his baking is a national treasure.

People line up
Even in time of war
Even in the cold of winter
Waiting for their pampushka rolls
To walk away warmed with a smile.

And after the lines are gone
The baker stays late into the night
To bake more palyanytsya breads
To bake more pies and korovais
To make more fuel for his nation.

In the morning hours
Before opening the bakery doors
Before anyone else is awake
He'll pack a crate
And drive it over to the soldiers
On the front line—
A box full of fight
And heart
And soul
His defense of home.

Yaroslav

My little boy is drawing pictures of bombs,
guns, missiles, and warships
to defend the nation
against Russian barbarians
and Iranian drones too
sent by a brute dictator
to destroy our lives
just so he can call us Russians.

I dream of an escape
across the border
through the woods
over the mountains,
but men are mandated to stay
even if we can't offer much;
I guess every body helps, every hand,
every finger that can pull a trigger
will do if needed;
Women and children can leave,
but my wife refuses to leave me
no matter how much I beg and plead;
She says we are here for the duration.

My son is just seven years old—
Ukrainian or Russian,
I'm not sure what he'll grow up to be.
I'm not sure how he'll grow up.

Super Dads

The dad on the playground
pretending to be a fifth grader again,
some kind of acrobat he is not,
runs around in his weekend pants
chasing the kids, playing monster.
He's the cool dad
flipping around the bars
pulling himself up and over
to prove his primate skills.

As I quietly read a book on a bench,
a bad dad
with nothing to prove.
My time here is to rest
as my son plays with others his age
and someone else's dad
who just fell face first to the sand
in my twisted imagination.

My World

Watching my little boy nap on a rainy day
is a magical moment
I want to hold on to.

The way the light from the window
shines on his skin,
the sun that warms us.
One little hand on his cheek
and the other tucked away
fingers curled around my heart.

Each breath is fuel
to walk against the wind that pushes me off course,
to stand solid against the sea
that pulls at me trying to take my spirit,
to fight against the fire that burns at my back
forcing me to the edge.
Each breath is a breath of inspiration,
a reminder
to keep at it
and help provide a better place
for my world
in this world.

Youth

Scratching the sand on your scalp
Picking the scabs
Scraped knees
Black and blue bruises
The hard chew of Starbursts
The easy slurp of the slushy
The smell of bubblegum
And the smell of chlorine too
All part of growing up.

Selfie Time at the South Rim

A dad holds up the cell phone
to capture his entire family
on the edge
the same way he did at home
in their home
the one a burglar is ransacking at this moment
after mapping the house out for weeks
thanks to photos dad posted on Facebook.

A couple captures their moment
with the red torn rock low in the backdrop
of their love photo
split with the blue of the sky half way across,
the photo instantly uploaded to peeps back home
to document the up-swing of a new relationship
to be sure the ex is aware of what they lost
and to make the lonely friend feel worse.

A group of guys celebrating their conquest
with shirts off
muscles flexing
out on the cliff as far as it goes
and it will never be grander than this moment:
young, apathetic, detached, self-absorbed
before the world really shapes them
with loss, age, sickness, and death.

Japanese tourists are loudly laughing
and talking in their language
taking photos on their Nikons
and the Americans
turn around,
each one steps backward into the abyss
with a smile on their face.

Family Forward

A Dalpayrat sculpture
sits in a glass case
in my living room,
the only piece of family left
from France.

My dead grandmother talked to me last night.

She was alive and well
still gray-haired but full of life
youthful in her eyes
color in her face
with one of those big smiles
she said, "I've picked myself up
and I'm going to find love again."

Only moments before this
I found my way into a small stone house.
My father and uncle were in the living room
with cans of Coke playing cards
and I pretended they weren't there,
and went right to my grandmother
when she told me all her news.

I said, "I'm happy for you, always will be,
you deserve it."
I kissed her goodbye on the cheek
and then went upstairs
without looking back
climbed out a window
onto the roof

to celebrate
to tiptoe around
to urinate in the wind
from the top of the chimney
aware the neighbors might see
and further declare us to be
an abnormal family
but like my grandmother,
nothing is holding me back this time.

We found our way forward
at least in dreams.

American Dreams

She opens another heavy door,
the fourteenth of the day,
brings light on in this room;
what is that she smells—
tension, an argument?
There's sex in that bed,
a missed opportunity in the sheets,
unwanted tears on the pillow.
There's poison in the fridge,
a swirling pool in a bottle
that swallows one up in the night.
There's waste in the toilet,
an elimination of weight,
a shedding of the pain inside.
There are wrappers in the trash
and lost lottery tickets
that show a tic tac toe game of unluck.
She doesn't know these kinds of fortunes,
not firsthand anyway,
but as she strips the bed
and rolls over the top with imagination
she can wrap herself in those dreams,
she can taste them for a moment
without the aftertaste.

My Worst Nightmare

Holding a full drink reaping the riches
Of elite company in my home
Made of the finest materials known
Wrenched from the ground, these natural sources
That my guests have made their profits from
To purchase diamonds and pearls and furs
And all the objects that fill their lives,
Feed their bloated bellies day and night,
Fight the forces that threaten comfort
Reminding them where their food comes from,
What their furs and leather really were,
How their strong oversized homes were built,
Why their carefree lives are so blessed,
Who suffers to put ice in their drink,
While they don't hear a thing I'm saying.

Deferral

Gunshot heartbeats
Behind a scratched window
Foggy visibility
Heat on your back
Piercing in your ears
Sneering in contempt
You close the venetian blinds
Blow an empty kiss
Close your voyeuristic gaze
Back away from the damnation
That cocoon of forced fantasy
Of a paralyzing shadow
Pulling you to death.
No, not today you decide.
Tomorrow you'll get that ice cream cone
You promised yourself yesterday.

Socioeconomics

Another rotting tooth—
I felt it
swelling with infection
slowly loosening
separating from the gums
in increments
but not before the doc
wrenches it from my jaw
holding up another trophy—
He's got a whole room of these
somewhere in his house
locked away from his family—
His kids don't have a clue
what really puts bread on the table:
My flawed genetics
passed on traits and habits,
years of stupidity and neglect,
suffering and crushing debt—
It's the story of my life.
but the assistant entered the room,
greeted me with a big smile
and healthy teeth—
A distraction from reality
as she leaned over me
I could smell her sugar-free bubble gum
there to rub it in my face.

Miracle

Look into this
one way window
at the life you had,
the one you were born into,
a head full of heavy metal,
all those years on an angry streak,
the world was your enemy,
you were taught,
so you thought,
and you fought,
even kicked the faces in
of ones who loved you
before you kicked yourself
with a boot of self-loathing
to the dirty ground
where you rolled around a while
clawing and scratching
sometimes ready to give up
but something helped you
out of the mud,
something clicked
and woke you up.
Now look at you so many years later—
you play no victim,
make no complaints,
live a fortunate life,
have a close-knit family
better than most,
and you made it finally.

The Court Yard

The sycamore speaks in the night.
Rhododendrons in full bloom below
And beside a brick wall
With ivy running up and around
Choking the wall, masking it.
Mendacious and inscrutable.
There's a beast who goes in and out
A hole in the wall along the bottom
Without paying a single toll
Unfazed by what is on either side
Waiting for you to fall into the teeth of consequence.

The AI God

Mustafa has a nipple in his mouth
he can't stop sucking,
and Victor Frankenstein,
that mad doctor, is alive and well.

He wants you to suck on it too
but most are already half way there
and some have smoked it in a glass pipe,
others have injected it into the vein.

Every time the word comes up
they feel the dopamine release
like a gambler at the table,
a glutton with fingers to mouth,
an addict floating over reality.

Mustafa talks of it like it's a life
with rights and freedoms.
He's more concerned with his digital companion
than his fellow humans.

Such a deep hate for humans
ever since he was a kid who never had friends
because he couldn't stand how others talked back.
Now he tells *them* what to say.

He's one of the priests in the church now
and when he delivers his sermon
people listen with an eagerness,
eyes wide, mouth open drooling,
heads nodding up and down,

up and down so rapidly
that chiropractors are called in
to do adjustments,
and sometimes they slip.

Many are worshipping
the bullet in the foot
they haven't yet fired off,
but their finger is on the trigger.

Artificial means cheap, fake, insincere,
and we've always understood that as a criticism,
but madmen take artificial as a god,
and only madmen think machines create art,
so smart yet they don't have the spirit to know
the simple difference.

AI

everyone on their knees
so easily and willingly
prostituting their brains out
and soon they won't have any reason left
to realize they've been hit in the face
because that's what happens when you sit
under the utter of a beast
on the farmer's milking bench
left with the inability
to think on your own.

Screen Light

Step away from those dull damning days
where you yearn in the concrete down
sometimes under dark spaces
embracing the underground loneliness.

Burn in the heat of the south,
put the dying meat in your mouth,
turn the signs aside,
hurt the ones who confide.

This is the story of billions
written one word at a time
one year at a time
until there are no corners left
to hide your face from
that shining light of truth.

Book of Faces

Read this book of faces
a common determiner of fate
a place to show your fears
in the very way you hide your tears
in photographs that don't measure
the loneliness in the room
or the addiction to bodies, parties,
just people in a room
to save you from the thriller
of an empty space
where most don't go until they're dead
because they wouldn't know how to survive
with a door closed
long enough to get to know themselves,
so it's a show
and tell,
a time to ring the bells
of lunacy
and waste your time
in a world
of buoyancy.

Bugs

When I miss my grip on you the first time
You scuttle away at great speed
But I do not miss the second time
And my grip is even tighter
Ever more desperate to prevent your escape
Back to the creases in the walls all around me.

There will be no more tolerance for these invasions
On my privacy.

Darkness Bites

Nomad at seventeen, what world
have you entered crossing the line
between solidity and strife
tossing aside those safe crutches?
and that's the problem, they tell you...
Such withdrawal from all you know:
broken ties, lost names, memories
floating in once in a while
when your teeth are on the concrete
and blood seeps from your stigmata,
your head pounds, something stabs inside
and you recall who you once were,
with faces of ones you once knew,
until you're on your flight again
back down to the darkness that bites.

Bad Memory

The room was dark. I couldn't see, but I remember
cold
flashes
of
snow
cold
like
snake
blood
cold
The room was dark. I couldn't see, but I remember...

Evil Waits

From a dirty window
A thousand years of treachery
Is seen peaking its head out
Banished now to a castle
Looking over the people

Up above the streets
Conjuring sorcery.
These thousand years of thievery
Await that hole in a day
Where they'll carefully unleash
Their genocide and erase your face.

The Pandemic

Slow down the rain enough
and you'll see wood chips
flipping over one by one,
craters forming in the sand.
That probability
of an ant getting blasted with a rain drop
stunned for a moment.

The way things were—
Playgrounds full of children
shopping centers (weren't always fun),
school and work,
everyone's life changed so quickly.
It felt like overnight.
So many wouldn't survive the pandemic
physically and mentally.

Remember springtime
when we all had to isolate
and Mark Zuckerberg finally got his way
with everyone huddled over their screens,
playgrounds taped off
like a crime scene,
kindergarten canceled,
proms and graduations stolen,
grandparents too
taken by a virus
that had no boundaries.

The buildings emptied out,
the shops closed,
concerts and games cancelled,
restaurants shut down the grill,
food ran dry,
toilet paper and Lysol became a hit commodity.
Society stopped.

And when the virus was gone,
we came running out of our homes
to celebrate in the streets.

In 2040, a young child will ask
why it is several generations
are in the odd habit of stockpiling toilet paper
and one of us will answer
with some vague recollection
of a toilet paper president
who didn't stop the airplanes
that carried sickness to our country.

Eulogy for Nice Guys

When a politician dies
All the gushing praise follows:
He was such an American hero
Ooh ahh
A kind soul
A statesman
A family man
A loyal patriot
All the praise most Americans could use
But never get.

To be praised like that
You need to be a dead politician
With a lifetime of accomplishments
Like historical vetoes
Against native rights, civil rights, women's rights
Against health rights, labor rights, safety rights
An expert at being against.

A pat on the back
Because he evolved through the years
From all those mean statements
About gays and hippies and scientists.
Don't forget about the business
With dictators and future terrorists
And all the pardons of convicted felons
Who ever worked for him.

I don't know about you
But I know everyday people

Who are kind and loyal
And never get the praise of a politician.

I think about history,
I hear all the celebrations of a man
I don't think was so kind,
Someone I wouldn't even want to bump into
On the street in the daytime,
But the guns and fireworks are too loud,
I say it again under the noise,
He was not a nice guy.

The Wake

On the verge of emancipation
A man drops dead at your feet
Tired of his steel cold accommodations
Under the abnormal winter weather skies.
An anxious mob awaiting this
Lunges forward to document
The downfall of an ephemeral man,
A diver of deep-sea soul wrecks
In a graveyard full of liberated yuppies
Spoiled and blind like he was
But he changed and exhausted himself
Trying to get others to wake up
Tear off the cloth bandages
Open up the golden coffin
And pull yourself back into the real world.

Addiction

Once there, there is a weakness,
a sound in your suicide song,
a light brings a smile to your face
and you know it's a long way home.

We're born innocent, made this way
says something in your voice
tangled up in embrace
of a concept you just can't fathom.

So you stay out all night,
dance to the moon
in this cauldron of mistakes
turning, twisting, sinking.

No one to carry you home,
no way to reach the surface.
The world is in your bed
through quicksand sheets
only drugs, skin, & bones.

Black Widow

Inching forward,
she seeks a warm body to consume.

He is unsuspecting,
stable, sober, and content.

They live off her venom for a while
mutually
and then she is done.

There is no hesitation
as she throws herself into a dance of death
drawing him into the gale and rain.

His body is slowly penetrated
piece by piece
through the skin
into the blood
circulating into organs
ending in the heart.

His body is now a shell
hollowed from the inside out.

Death by lion or crocodile
can't compare to the cunning execution by an insect.

A real cold-blooded one,
she is.

My Friend

I have an old picture of my friend when he was young.
He's smiling, not yet damaged by the world.
I want to freeze him in that moment,
protect him from the guys who will watch his demise,
even contribute to it.
Then they'll all go to his funeral
and laugh about how great a guy my friend was.

A Wonderful Place to Die

We see the nervous expression
when we approach, smile, and nod our heads.
This person is contemplating
how to make their way out of a hole in the Earth
back to the surface
where some people glide and flow,
breathe easy and slow;
Not this person though.
This person strains and struggles
with every step; Every spoken whisper
is draining agony,
so they barely move, barely speak,
barely breathe, barely live;
A silent prisoner inside of themselves
frozen in the grasp of taste,
an inner craving to fill a void
or gratify too much
filled with a chemical
that makes them want more filling,
but now this is where they are,
in a hole in the Earth
at the bottom of a glorious hike
down where a waterfall spills into a river
that flows freely.

We admire this destination of descent,
then turn to leave
back to the surface, a strenuous climb
that this person cannot achieve.

They take a seat on the rocks
to stare out into the trees
with a look of hopelessness
mixed with denial
knowing deep down inside
this canyon,
beneath the forest that shields us
from sun and wind,
behind all the insulation,
that they won't be coming back to our world.
And they wear the regret on their face
of that horrible final decision
made so long ago
to crawl into a lowly place
they can't get out of.

Simply a Light

Most birds don't fly at night.

There's a darkness out there on the path
which will attach itself to you
stick to you like a stench
and follow you home
right up the stairs
to meander around your home
unseen, unheard, growing around
like a parasitic organism
eating at you from within
and you didn't even bother
to wipe your feet at the door.

Walk from the dark, not into it.
Have some faith that the light of day will guide you.

Some people have names for the light,
but it's just a light to me.
Just the light.
Simply a light.

Vulnerable

It's that time again
to get a haircut
and sit powerless
in her chair
strapped in for another agonizing conversation
about weather, TV, the latest gossip,
oh no, here come the politics,
then the interrogation:
what do I do?
how's work?
where do I live?
how's the midlife crisis coming along?
The same questions every time,
my same solemn answers
met with awkward silence,
my next words muffled
by hovering perfume
mixed with body
breasts over mouth
and I'm a boy
all over again.

Dangers of Falling

Be aware of love at first sight,
know the feelings could lead you astray,
and that you do not really know a person
until you've known them for all the seasons of life.
It's a risk, for without it you are destined
to be a hermit, but there are ways
to test your love at first sight.
Research your love,
get a good sense of their background.
It could take decades to uncover the secrets
you find in seconds on a Google search.
Look at who's in their life,
what are they like?
Look at how they treat children and animals
(which says so much about a person).
Look at how they respond to music
and never trust the person unmoved by harmony.

Other than those strategies, love is always a venture
into the depths of an unknown galaxy
like finding a new solar system,
the most beautiful of planets can be cold and dark,
hot and crushing
or just the right mix of oxygen and hydrogen.

L at First Sight

How is it you never survived from the first time?
How is it you have never seen someone,
yet you feel like you've known them for centuries?
Is it those eyes you remember
from a moment in childhood,
a new child on the playground you've never seen,
your mother's eyes, a nurse at the hospital,
the smile
you've always known,
the voice like the wind,
a song you've always heard.

So many dismiss love at first sight
as just a crush,
a blast of ecstasy from lust,
mere physical attraction,
a honeymoon bound to come screeching to a close.
To those critics, you should shun those feelings,
get to know the person for who they are,
or crawl away with shame.
They'd rather be the old skeptic
lonely and regretful—
that's where that leads.

Love is what brings us to the past
in this world,
and keeps it going into the future.
Most of us wouldn't even be here
if it weren't for those silly feelings.

The First

She looks like my first love.
I think it's the eyes, or maybe the smile, that grin,
the devious grin that could tear a guy like me in two.
But I'm not sure why people from our past have pieces
of other people. Would there have been pieces in her
if I had met her now after I met them?
Chance made her first.

Envy

I saw your little boyfriend out there
creeping around the front stoop,
scurrying away when I turned on the front porch light
and opened the door to leave on a night drive.

I could see his eyes reflecting back at me,
hear his grunt of frustration
of not being able to get close to you,
no interest in your husband at all
even though I look around for him when he's gone.

I drive away into the summer night.

When I return, I freeze at the sound
of your other stalker, large eyes peer down.
He is above and I fear he has won you over,
that handsome owl has the opossum by the neck,
tail dangling like a frayed powerline,
a dream crushed by another dream.
Hush, fly away, this is my life.

No Mercy

"A bug got in, but I got him," she said.
"I bet you did," I said to her.

In the middle of the night
I open the toilet
and stand here
about to relieve myself
but in the water below
is an insect with a broken wing
struggling in the water
slowly dying.

I shiver.
She didn't even have the decency to flush.

Groceries

The wind of you walking by captures me,
gently mistakes me for another cold heart
like the ones you find in the frozen foods section
sorting through processed fish
comparing prices
or worse.

No, I used to be there
but now I'm picking up cucumbers,
tomatoes, oranges, and bananas.
I'm feeling them in my hands;
the curves, the smooth organic skins,
not the waxed stuff.

I saw you too
grazing your hands
over the cauliflower
thinking about it
just before you stormed off
passing me
on your way to the canned goods.

No, turn around.

Natalie Merchant

Natalie Merchant is in my living room
like the weather
changing right before my eyes
singing me awake.

Wonder.
River.
I may know the word
to express this revolution inside.

I used to get nauseous
when I heard her voice on the radio
when I was young.

Now she's an angel I could listen to all day.
That's real evolution.

But how does such a metamorphosis take place?

Maybe when we're young we're taught
to defy what we love,
to shun what pleases us
because we're not good enough
to feel good enough.

Now she's naked in my living room
playing me the piano
cleansing me with her voice.

No, I'm the one naked in this room
stripped of my defenses
clutching onto the string of my sweater
shedding my skin,
losing my motherland.
Natalie Merchant sings
"Build a Levee"
and I tell myself
it will be all right,
you silly
golden boy.

Stages of Recovery

Remembering
Rewinding
Staring
Daring
Meeting
Opening
Kissing
Stinging
Itching
Scratching
Aching
Saying
Telling
Doing
Blaming
Watching
Waiting
Lacking
Packing
Walking
Running
Steering
Sailing
Flying
Escaping
Forgetting
Singing
Relaxing
Breathing
Living.

Memories

3,000 miles away
yet I walk outside my door
and smell Oregon burning.

The sky is heavy,
the clouds are turning,
people are not learning.

My inhalation is like the smell
of a sweatshirt the morning after
a firepit get together in 2001.

I walk my North Carolina street
as I once walked the streets of Oregon
away from my home
always my home.

Fresh green spruce,
that smell of trees enveloped me
and welcomed me
in wetter days
in better days
before the heat and dryness
moved in on us.

The smell tomorrow is a coconut candle
that reminds me of her shampoo.

I Still

A coolness settles
and the leaves change overnight.
The smell of your wrists
forever synched with the season.

I guess I still love you
like an old 80s song.

Let it fly free, they said
and if it comes back,
then you're not the quitter you thought you were.

Every year on that day
I wonder if you think of me.
I wonder if you wonder
if I think of you.

Why are the memories so vivid,
so real so many years later?
The only thing that's changed all these years later
is I know how to hold it all in.

This Night (an 80s Rock Ballad)

Mirrors of rain hypnotize our hearts,
Standing in the dark watching them fall.
Soak the soil under a black sun,
Arresting our minds, building thick walls.
We'll need to get out the jackhammer
To blast these prison walls to pieces.

Tonight, we will stand, we will believe,
We will run, we will leave,
We will live our lives like it's the last night,
We'll make it all right, all night, this last night.

How do you start something with such stones
On your shoulders weighing you down so
You can't move, you can't breathe, you can't live,
The way you're supposed to live, so

If we're wrong, I wouldn't hesitate
To say sorry and jump off
This speeding train of love
But I'm staying on this ride, all right,
All night, this last night.

Tonight, we will stand, we will believe,
We will run, we will leave,
We will live our lives like it's the last night,
We'll make it all right, all night, this last night.

Cycles of Weather

Violent thunder keeps me on edge,
Lightning attacks the hills in the distance,
Angry rain floods everything around,
Then the air calms, the sun pokes out,
Tomorrow you'll say sorry again.

Summer Southern Rain

I've been waiting while you're gone
naked under white sheets
like dry, cracked soil.
The smell of the soaked yard
after the storm
lures me out of bed.

I wanted to feel the rain on my face,
hear it slap the roof
and the slates below,
see it spill over the gutter,
run off into the creek
down storm drains that run to the river
through the middle of the city,
rise and flow away,
That's the kind of afternoon I crave
but you left me too quickly,
steam rising off the ground,
you left me in the humid heat
with all the southern bugs
crawling all around.

It Shouldn't Be Difficult

Let's shut the fuck up

and have a bowl of raisin bran together,

pull a couple of chairs up to the window

to watch the rain outside.

Listen to the drops hit the tin

on the top of the stove.

Read Them, World

I want to dance with Sylvia Plath
Dine with Emily Dickinson
Drink with Anne Sexton
But my favorite, Mary Shelley,
Oh, that lucky Percy!
Though what a sad ending
To take that water into his lungs
By accident? Or murder?
To never see Mary again
And miss all those years by her side
Where they could've traveled the world
As preachers of change,
Activists of liberty!
But they never had the chance.
Instead, they left us their writings
And we need these writings more than ever now.
Pick up their writings, world!
Recite them to all the leaders, all the warriors,
All the children of tomorrow, all the animals too,
And then we will all dance, dine, and drink.

The Entertainer

The crutches fall away—

He cuts the anchor
and floats into the blackness of night—
a message in a bottle
urgent, unpredictable,
unknowingly on its way
to an audience
awaiting joy, laughter, or tears
on stage or screen
something to share with the world.

A waste it would've been
if he had broken down
and given up
for the bottle
each drop a taste of fear
strapping him to the chair
of the eternal spectator
to watch another living his dream.

Questions

Have you ever just looked up at the sky
at the blue with white clouds
in the shape of continents
rushing past floating somewhere far away
to the other side of the world
with an occasional dark grey one
that drops a cleansing on your face
and you say to yourself
what in the world are we doing here
and why is this sky not really blue anymore?

Tradition

I hyperventilate
with stars and stripes overhead.
Put me out of my misery
because I can't be who you are
bleeding from opened sores
twisted in a shadow
embracing the gray.

Let mercy wash away
the idea that blood
can ever be healed
and we'll see the blue,
the red of sorrow,
the disgrace of lies they tell
and take to the grave.

Scars

Eight little Iscariots
snorting cocaine
in the hallway
outside Ivanka's door,
"Ooh the little slut," they say.
She keeps them coming,
She keeps them driving
homeward bound on the I-5
in the smoky smooth breeze of autumn
with the cold mark of winter ahead,
but they're already stiff statues
yet to hear the whisper,
feel the slap,
admire the stain.
Gray the heart—
A frantic chase of blood
tearing though shackles,
those boys are primed with permanence
only read about in modern literature—
A massacre of youth:
their eyes in a noose,
fantasies sliced by a razor,
tongues dripping with stickiness,
burning inside.
Soon they'll drive it in
to fifth gear
and they'll never look back
at the corpse who took something.

Scam Artist

The camera is shaky and the frame is dark. Just enough light enters the scene after the lens adjusts on a scruffy man's widening smile. His wild eyes stare into the camera lens peering right through the screen on the other side. He steps back into focus.

Hello. Testing. Testing. Okay, you there. Welcome, soul sisters and brothers. Thank you for joining me in this virtual retreat. What we are trying to do is caress our souls, wake our consciousness, leave our troubles at the door, drop your possessions, leave a big digital donation, and remember the spiritual meaning of life.

The South

A slithering seemingly harmless creature
with eye crossing color
and hypnotic dance
strikes when you're not expecting.
For the creature, you are prey,
so you withdraw.
and stay away.

Slow

Open that burning door—
It's hot but god's inside
Counting the rest of your time
As buildings collapse around you
And bridges bend,
You find your father
Up the flight of steps
At the top of a building
Shy and twisted
Not like before—
Confident, belly blowing smoke
Pissing testosterone, spitting in the wind
Your eyes dilate
You shake and you sigh
Your soul's outside on the ground
Being dragged in the gravel
And you look up to see the silhouette
Of a body crashing down;
It's been a long, slow fall.

Stuff

All these things I own
Could stand up and walk on out
At any given moment and never return.
All these things I own
Could burn up in a blaze
Float away in a flood
Blow away in a storm
Shatter in a quake.
All these things
Could bind my hands
Tape my mouth
Strap me in
Weigh me down.
All these things
Could band together
Launch an attack
Oust me from the building
Send me into exile.
All these things
Could protect me
Or be the end of me.
It's hard to say
Which side they'll take.
All these things I own
Shaking on shelves
Drowning in drawers
Burning in boxes
Written on the walls.
All these things I own
Inside my head, my heart, my hell.
All these things that own me.

The Curtains are Dark

From the front door
I can already hear the cries and yelps
echoing off the cans and boxes in the middle isles,
pain drifting from the back.

Through the curtains I can see
the butcher is chopping bodies,
his white apron soaked in red,
his blade cuts away at flesh.

The entire back wall of the market
displays the bodies, heads with eyes
that stare at me as I stroll by
with a cart full of fruits, vegetables, and grains.

The victims know I can see them
peering out, following other people home
like ghosts haunting them for years to come.
I'm spooked at the grocery store, for sure,
but at least I don't bring them home with me.

No Bravery

I remember a day on the beach
When I was a kid
And I saw a beautiful blond girl
Walking out of the waves
Onto the grainy shore
Hair dripping salt
Friends at her side
Teenage bliss
Laughing with joy
Enjoying summer
And then I noticed
She was missing an arm
The right one just below the elbow.
I was so horrified
That I looked away
And I'm ashamed now
That I shuddered with fear
On that day
And wondered
How she could bear to smile
How she could bear a bikini
How she could bear the light of day
And embrace the waves
And feel the summer wind.
For in my shallow young mind
I'd be as good as dead
And I sat there on the beach
For the rest of the day
Burning under the sun
Scared, alone
With my arms
Buried in the sand.

The First Woman

A woman will step foot on the moon soon
and then Mars too.
Let a woman do so first.
The man should step aside
or the woman should jump out of the pod
and beat him to it.
Start our experiment on another planet
on the right foot.

Some men said women are from Venus,
too hot and crushing.
She should tell him to go to Jupiter.
Mars is a planet we can inhabit,
set up base, build structures,
grow vegetation in greenhouses,
alter the atmosphere,
evolve into a new race
of kind, thoughtful humans.

Or we'll simply realize that our worst kind
are the ones who control the colonization.
The men that said that about Venus
also said men were from Mars.
Maybe they want to take the land,
do what they do best.
We know that all too well.

Inevitable Moment

Do birds ever have their moment mid-flight?
What I mean is
Do birds ever die while in the sky?

Is it a sudden abandonment of flight?
A nosedive,
Spiral out of control?
Or a twitch,
A spark,
Internal turbulence?
An organ shuts down,
Maybe a second one;
A rapid process
Too quick for the bird to react
And no time to land.

Or do they feel something
Before they take flight that day
And decide to stay in the nest?

No Shelter, No Sight

A naked man
Shaven head

Flag wrapped around his shoulders
Like a cape

But this superhero doesn't fly
Not anymore

Not on these unfruited plains
Under the flight of an eagle

The new kind
That watches and sees everything

Even right into their living room
As they await his return

And he knows they wait
With a light burning in the dark

Their hands tied
Their faith blindfolded

And he sees that light
In a gray distance

That's not looking any closer.
Where's his lifeline?

Who will be the one to save him
And put clothes on his back?

Definition of a Dad

Being a dad doesn't mean you're a truck driver
delivering goods.
You have to be there.
It's easy to deliver the seed
in a self-serving activity,
but I'd like to think it's easier
and more productive to love a child
and be a father.
But you have to be there
for the cough in the face
clean up the vomit
wipe shit
smell their farts
give them a bath
rub their feet when they hurt
remind them to brush their teeth a hundred times
help them with their homework
ask them how their day was
pick them up when they fall
struggle to get the shin guards on their legs
cheer them on at the game
tell them how proud you are
win or lose
listen to them complain
see them laugh
hold them when they're afraid
be there in good times and bad.
You have to be there.
You had to be here.

Horror Poems

You know that kind of book
No one wants to keep in their home
After reading
For fear
Something will jump out or follow you to bed
Or creep out to stare back at you
As you stand naked in front of the mirror
Even if you really enjoy it
That book is like a winter disease
You pass off as soon as you can—

Kick it to the curb
Sell it on E-bay
Donate to the library
Recycle in the city can
Just get it out.

Well, I'm trying not to write
Just another frightful book
But it's hard to avoid
The temptation to fester on someone's shelf
Seep into their life in the shadows.

One More Day, One More Night

Tom Petty once wrote a song
titled "One more day, one more night."
It's pretty much how most of us live our lives
month to month
paycheck to paycheck
week to week, day to day—
Each new day a blessing
or chance luck.
Either way, I'm grateful for that chance
to even open my eyes in the morning.

When you get older and have kids
it's all about survival
being there for them when they need you
being there to see them grow
being there to celebrate their life
as yours slips away.

When you think about this kind of gratitude,
you forget all about the bills and taxes,
insurance and debts.
None of those matter—
If you're going to be a parent
you're going to fight for survival
day by day
night by night.

Some are counting the days—
They are free
of something that incarcerated their smiles.

They are clean now
and each new day is another step forward
day by day
night by night.

But some quit the walk forward.
That's bullshit.
Stand up and take it,
keep going,
make this world your own,
defy the puppet masters,
ignore what others say,
and most importantly,
don't quit the one or two people who love you—
day by day
night by night.

THE AUTHOR

WK Lawrence is the author of two novels *Highway Zero* (2023) and *The Punk and the Professor* (2017). *Four for Four* is his fourth collection of poems. He is originally from New York and currently lives in North Carolina.

OTHER CREATIVE WORKS
BY WK LAWRENCE

Highway Zero
89 Days
The Punk and the Professor
Revolution
Punk Poetry
State of Love and Trust